Unraveling The Mind: Understanding OCD, Autism, And Obsession

Travis Breeding

Published by Travis Breeding, 2024.

While every precaution has been taken in the preparation of this book, the publisher assumes no responsibility for errors or omissions, or for damages resulting from the use of the information contained herein.

UNRAVELING THE MIND: UNDERSTANDING OCD, AUTISM, AND OBSESSION

First edition. February 20, 2024.

Copyright © 2024 Travis Breeding.

ISBN: 979-8224474868

Written by Travis Breeding.

Also by Travis Breeding

Harmony in Flux: Navigating Bi-Polar Brilliance
The Friendship Rainbow
The Great Kindergarten Adventure: A Story about Going to School with Autism
The Magic Forest Adventure
Unlocking Brilliance: Navigating Autism and Applied Behavior Analysis Towards a Radiant Future
Decoding Love: Navigating Dating and Relationships on the Autism Spectrum
Echoes of a Late Diagnosis: Unveiling the Spectrum Within
From Theory to Practice: Implementing Effective Autism Interventions
St
The Amazing Adventures of Aiden and His Asperger's Superpowers
The Magical Adventures of Lily and the Enchanted Forest
Unlocking Potential: A Journey Of Discovery Through ABA Therapy
Unlocking Potential: Navigating Employment for Neurodiverse Talent
Unlocking the Spectrum: A Journey through Applied Behavior Analysis from an Autistic Perspective
Unlocking The Spectrum: Navigating The Complexity Of Autism With Advanced Strategies And Insights
Beyond The Spectrum: Insights From Autistic Adults
Beyond The Stereotypes
Breaking Barriers: Navigating Autism With Therapeutic Insight
Celebrating Neurodiversity
Embracing Differences

From Diagnosis To Treatment
From Dreams To Reality: The Young President
Living With Autism: A Journey Of Triumph And Challenges
Neurodiversity Unveiled: Navigating The Spectrum Of Inclusion
Sunshine At Disney World
The Art Of Reinforcement
The Magical School Bus Ride: A Journey Of Understanding
ThroughThe Spectrum Of Love
Dancing With Shadows: How To Turn Your Fears Into Powerful Allies
From Chaos To Control: How To Develop Strong Executive
functioning Skills
From Misunderstood To Mainstream
Unlocking the Spectrum: A Comprehensive Guide to Understanding
and Thriving with Autism
Unraveling The Mind: Understanding OCD, Autism, And Obsession

Table of Contents

Chapter 1: The Power of Inclusion: Supporting Individuals with Autism

Autism Spectrum Disorder (ASD) is a neurodevelopmental disorder that affects individuals' social communication and interaction skills. It is characterized by a range of behaviors and challenges, making it a complex disorder to understand and support. It is estimated that 1 in 54 children in the United States are diagnosed with ASD, highlighting the importance of understanding and supporting individuals with this disorder.

Understanding and supporting individuals with ASD is crucial for several reasons. Firstly, it allows for the creation of inclusive environments where individuals with ASD can thrive and reach their full potential. Secondly, it promotes empathy and understanding among neurotypical individuals, fostering a more inclusive society. Lastly, it ensures that individuals with ASD have access to the necessary resources and support systems to lead fulfilling lives.

Understanding Autism Spectrum Disorder: What You Need to Know

ASD is a developmental disorder that affects individuals' social communication and interaction skills. It is characterized by difficulties in social interaction, communication, and repetitive behaviors. Individuals with ASD may have challenges in understanding nonverbal cues, maintaining eye contact, engaging in reciprocal conversations, and developing friendships.

Diagnosing ASD can be complex as it is a spectrum disorder, meaning that individuals can exhibit a wide range of symptoms and behaviors. The Diagnostic and Statistical Manual of Mental Disorders

(DSM-5) outlines specific criteria for diagnosing ASD, including deficits in social communication and interaction, restricted interests or repetitive behaviors, and symptoms that are present in early childhood.

The prevalence of ASD has been increasing over the years, with more children being diagnosed with the disorder. According to the Centers for Disease Control and Prevention (CDC), approximately 1 in 54 children in the United States are diagnosed with ASD. This increase in prevalence highlights the need for increased awareness, understanding, and support for individuals with ASD.

The Importance of Inclusion for Individuals with Autism

Inclusion refers to the practice of ensuring that individuals with disabilities, including those with ASD, are fully included in all aspects of society. Inclusion is crucial for individuals with ASD as it provides them with opportunities to develop social skills, build relationships, and access education and employment.

Inclusion has numerous benefits for individuals with ASD. Firstly, it promotes social interaction and communication skills, allowing individuals to develop meaningful relationships and connections. It also provides opportunities for individuals with ASD to learn from their neurotypical peers and vice versa, fostering a sense of empathy and understanding.

Exclusion and isolation can have negative effects on individuals with ASD. It can lead to feelings of loneliness, low self-esteem, and increased anxiety. Inclusive environments, on the other hand, promote a sense of belonging and acceptance, which can have a positive impact on individuals' mental health and overall well-being.

Individuals with disabilities, including those with ASD, are protected by various legal rights and protections. The Individuals with

Disabilities Education Act (IDEA) ensures that individuals with disabilities have access to a free appropriate public education (FAPE) in the least restrictive environment (LRE). This means that individuals with ASD should be educated alongside their neurotypical peers to the maximum extent possible.

Common Challenges Faced by Individuals with Autism

Individuals with ASD face various challenges that can impact their daily lives and functioning. These challenges include sensory processing difficulties, communication challenges, social skills deficits, and executive functioning difficulties.

Sensory processing difficulties refer to difficulties in processing and responding to sensory information from the environment. Individuals with ASD may be hypersensitive or hyposensitive to certain sensory stimuli such as noise, light, touch, or smell. This can lead to sensory overload or sensory seeking behaviors.

Communication challenges are another common characteristic of ASD. Individuals with ASD may have difficulties in understanding and using verbal and nonverbal communication. They may have limited vocabulary, struggle with expressive language, or have challenges in understanding social cues and gestures.

Social skills deficits are also common in individuals with ASD. They may have difficulties in initiating and maintaining conversations, understanding social norms and expectations, and developing friendships. This can lead to social isolation and difficulties in forming meaningful relationships.

Executive functioning difficulties refer to challenges in planning, organizing, and completing tasks. Individuals with ASD may struggle with time management, organization, and problem-solving skills. This can impact their academic performance, daily routines, and overall independence.

Strategies for Creating an Inclusive Environment

Creating an inclusive environment for individuals with ASD requires a multi-faceted approach that addresses their unique needs and challenges. Some strategies for creating an inclusive environment include implementing universal design for learning, using positive behavior supports, adopting a collaborative team approach, and providing assistive technology and accommodations.

Universal design for learning (UDL) is an educational framework that aims to provide multiple means of representation, expression, and engagement to meet the diverse needs of learners. By implementing UDL principles, educators can create inclusive classrooms where individuals with ASD can access the curriculum and participate fully in learning activities.

Positive behavior supports (PBS) is a proactive approach to managing challenging behaviors. It focuses on teaching individuals with ASD appropriate behaviors and providing them with the necessary supports to succeed. PBS strategies include using visual supports, implementing structured routines, and providing clear expectations and consequences.

Adopting a collaborative team approach involves involving various stakeholders in the individual's life, including parents, educators, therapists, and support staff. By working together as a team, individuals with ASD can receive consistent support across different settings and have their unique needs addressed effectively.

Assistive technology and accommodations can also play a crucial role in creating an inclusive environment for individuals with ASD.

Assistive technology such as communication devices or visual supports can enhance communication skills and independence. Accommodations such as preferential seating or extra time on tasks can help individuals with ASD succeed in academic and social settings.

Building Positive Relationships with Individuals with Autism

Building positive relationships with individuals with ASD is essential for their overall well-being and development. It requires a person-centered approach, empathy and understanding, positive reinforcement and praise, and active listening and communication.

A person-centered approach involves recognizing and valuing the unique strengths, interests, and needs of individuals with ASD. It involves actively involving them in decision-making processes and respecting their autonomy and preferences. By taking a person-centered approach, individuals with ASD can feel empowered and supported.

Empathy and understanding are crucial when building relationships with individuals with ASD. It involves putting oneself in their shoes, recognizing their challenges, and responding with compassion and patience. By demonstrating empathy and understanding, individuals with ASD can feel accepted and valued.

Positive reinforcement and praise are effective strategies for building positive relationships with individuals with ASD. By providing specific praise and rewards for desired behaviors, individuals with ASD can feel motivated and encouraged to continue engaging in those behaviors. This can help build their self-esteem and confidence.

Active listening and communication involve actively engaging in conversations with individuals with ASD, using clear and concise language, and providing opportunities for them to express themselves.

By actively listening to their thoughts, feelings, and ideas, individuals with ASD can feel heard and understood.

The Role of Communication in Supporting Individuals with Autism

Communication plays a crucial role in supporting individuals with ASD. It involves using augmentative and alternative communication (AAC), visual supports and schedules, social stories and scripts, and clear and concise language.

Augmentative and alternative communication (AAC) refers to the use of tools or strategies to support communication for individuals who have difficulties with speech or language. AAC can include sign language, picture exchange systems, or electronic devices that generate speech. By using AAC, individuals with ASD can effectively communicate their wants, needs, and thoughts.

Visual supports such as visual schedules or visual cues can help individuals with ASD understand and follow routines and expectations. Visual supports provide a visual representation of information, making it easier for individuals with ASD to process and understand.

Social stories and scripts are narrative tools that can help individuals with ASD navigate social situations and understand social norms and expectations. Social stories provide a step-by-step guide to specific social situations, while scripts provide pre-determined responses or phrases for common social interactions.

Using clear and concise language is important when communicating with individuals with ASD. It involves using simple and concrete language, avoiding figurative language or idioms, and providing visual supports when necessary. By using clear and concise language, individuals with ASD can better understand and respond to communication.

Teaching Self-Advocacy Skills to Individuals with Autism

Teaching self-advocacy skills to individuals with ASD is crucial for their independence and self-determination. It involves teaching self-determination and decision-making skills, encouraging self-expression and self-awareness, and supporting self-advocacy in the community.

Self-advocacy refers to the ability to speak up for oneself, make decisions, and advocate for one's own needs and rights. Teaching self-determination skills involves helping individuals with ASD identify their strengths, interests, and goals, and develop the skills necessary to make informed decisions.

Encouraging self-expression and self-awareness involves providing opportunities for individuals with ASD to express their thoughts, feelings, and preferences. This can be done through various means such as art therapy, journaling, or role-playing. By encouraging self-expression and self-awareness, individuals with ASD can develop a sense of identity and agency.

Supporting self-advocacy in the community involves providing individuals with ASD with the necessary skills and resources to advocate for themselves in various settings. This can include teaching them how to communicate their needs effectively, educating them about their rights and protections, and connecting them with support networks or organizations.

Supporting Social Skills Development for Individuals with Autism

Supporting social skills development is crucial for individuals with ASD to navigate social interactions and build meaningful relationships. Some strategies for supporting social skills development include social skills training and coaching, peer-mediated interventions, social stories and role-playing, and community-based instruction and practice.

Social skills training and coaching involve teaching individuals with ASD specific social skills through structured lessons and practice. This can include teaching them how to initiate conversations, take turns, or interpret nonverbal cues. By providing explicit instruction and opportunities for practice, individuals with ASD can develop their social skills.

Peer-mediated interventions involve pairing individuals with ASD with neurotypical peers who can serve as social mentors or coaches. This allows individuals with ASD to learn from their peers and receive feedback and support in real-life social situations. Peer-mediated interventions can be implemented in various settings such as schools or community programs.

Social stories and role-playing are effective tools for teaching individuals with ASD appropriate social behaviors and responses. Social stories provide a narrative description of a specific social situation, while role-playing allows individuals to practice and rehearse appropriate behaviors. By using social stories and role-playing, individuals with ASD can develop their social skills in a safe and structured environment.

Community-based instruction and practice involve providing individuals with ASD with opportunities to practice their social skills in real-life settings. This can include community outings, volunteer work, or job training programs. By practicing their social skills in authentic contexts, individuals with ASD can generalize their skills to different situations.

Addressing Sensory Needs of Individuals with Autism

Addressing the sensory needs of individuals with ASD is crucial for their comfort and well-being. Some strategies for addressing sensory needs include sensory integration therapy, environmental modifications, sensory diets and routines, and collaborative problem-solving.

Sensory integration therapy is a therapeutic approach that aims to help individuals with ASD regulate their sensory responses. It involves engaging in activities that provide sensory input, such as swinging, jumping, or playing with textured materials. Sensory integration therapy can help individuals with ASD better process and respond to sensory stimuli.

Environmental modifications involve making changes to the physical environment to accommodate the sensory needs of individuals with ASD. This can include reducing noise levels, providing visual supports, or creating designated quiet spaces. By modifying the environment, individuals with ASD can feel more comfortable and better able to focus and engage.

Sensory diets and routines involve providing individuals with ASD with a structured schedule of sensory activities throughout the day. This can include activities that provide sensory input, such as deep pressure or movement breaks. By incorporating sensory activities into their daily routines, individuals with ASD can regulate their sensory responses and maintain optimal arousal levels.

Collaborative problem-solving involves working together with individuals with ASD to identify their specific sensory needs and develop strategies to address them. This can involve using visual supports to communicate preferences, providing choices for sensory activities, or implementing individualized accommodations. By involving individuals with ASD in the problem-solving process, their unique needs can be effectively addressed.

The Benefits of Inclusion for Neurotypical Peers

Inclusion not only benefits individuals with ASD but also has positive effects on their neurotypical peers. Some benefits of inclusion for neurotypical peers include increased empathy and understanding, improved social skills and relationships, enhanced academic and cognitive outcomes, and a positive impact on school culture and climate.

Inclusion provides neurotypical peers with opportunities to interact and build relationships with individuals with ASD. This exposure fosters empathy and understanding, as neurotypical peers learn about the unique challenges and strengths of individuals with ASD. It also promotes acceptance and reduces stigma surrounding disabilities.

Interacting with individuals with ASD can also improve neurotypical peers' social skills and relationships. It provides opportunities for them to practice patience, tolerance, and effective communication. It also encourages the development of inclusive attitudes and behaviors, which can benefit their relationships with individuals from diverse backgrounds.

Inclusive classrooms have been shown to have positive effects on academic and cognitive outcomes for neurotypical peers. Research has found that inclusive classrooms promote higher levels of engagement, motivation, and academic achievement. This is attributed to the diverse perspectives and learning styles present in inclusive classrooms.

Inclusive environments also have a positive impact on school culture and climate. They promote a sense of belonging and acceptance among all students, fostering a positive and supportive learning environment. Inclusive schools are more likely to have lower rates of bullying and higher levels of student satisfaction.

Advocating for Inclusion: How You Can Make a Difference

Advocating for inclusion is crucial for promoting the rights and well-being of individuals with ASD. There are several ways in which individuals can make a difference, including educating others about ASD and inclusion, advocating for policy and legislative changes, supporting inclusive practices in schools and communities, and volunteering and supporting organizations that promote inclusion.

Educating others about ASD and inclusion is an important first step in promoting understanding and acceptance. This can be done through sharing personal experiences, organizing awareness campaigns or events, or providing resources and information to others. By educating others, individuals can help dispel myths and misconceptions surrounding ASD.

Advocating for policy and legislative changes is another effective way to promote inclusion. This can involve contacting elected officials, participating in advocacy groups or organizations, or supporting initiatives that promote the rights of individuals with disabilities. By advocating for policy changes, individuals can help create a more inclusive society by pushing for laws and regulations that protect the rights and ensure the equal opportunities of individuals with disabilities. This can include advocating for accessible infrastructure, inclusive education, employment opportunities, healthcare access, and social inclusion. By actively engaging in policy advocacy, individuals can contribute to dismantling barriers and promoting a society that values and includes people of all abilities.

Chapter 2: Why Intersectionality Matters: Understanding the Complexities of Identity

Intersectionality is a concept that has gained significant attention in recent years, particularly within feminist discourse. It refers to the interconnected nature of social categorizations such as race, gender, class, and sexuality, and how they overlap and intersect to create unique experiences of oppression and privilege. Intersectionality recognizes that individuals hold multiple identities and that these identities cannot be separated or understood in isolation from one another. It is a crucial framework for understanding the complexities of power dynamics and social inequality, and it is essential for creating a more inclusive and equitable society.

The Basics of Intersectionality: What It Is and Why It Matters

Intersectionality can be defined as the recognition of how different forms of oppression, discrimination, and privilege intersect and interact with one another. It acknowledges that individuals experience multiple forms of marginalization or privilege simultaneously, and that these experiences are shaped by the intersections of their various identities. For example, a woman of color may face both racism and sexism, which can compound her experiences of discrimination and oppression.

The importance of intersectionality lies in its ability to challenge the notion that social issues can be understood or addressed in isolation from one another. By recognizing the interconnected nature of social categorizations, intersectionality allows for a more nuanced understanding of power dynamics and social inequality. It highlights the ways in which different forms of oppression reinforce and perpetuate one another, and it calls for a more inclusive approach to activism and social justice.

The History of Intersectionality: How It Emerged as a Framework for Understanding Identity

Intersectionality emerged as a framework for understanding identity in the late 20th century, primarily within Black feminist theory. Kimberlé Crenshaw, a legal scholar and critical race theorist, is credited with coining the term "intersectionality" in 1989. Crenshaw argued that traditional feminist theory failed to adequately address the experiences of Black women because it focused primarily on gender while neglecting the ways in which race intersects with gender to shape their experiences.

Crenshaw's work was groundbreaking in highlighting the unique experiences of Black women and the need for an intersectional approach to feminism. Since then, intersectionality has evolved and expanded within feminist discourse to include other forms of identity such as class, sexuality, disability, religion, age, and nationality. It has become a crucial tool for understanding the complexities of social inequality and for advocating for a more inclusive and equitable society.

The Intersectionality of Race and Gender: Examining the Overlapping Identities of Women of Color

Women of color face unique experiences that are shaped by the intersection of race and gender. They often face both racism and sexism, which can compound their experiences of discrimination and oppression. For example, Black women may face stereotypes that portray them as hypersexual or aggressive, which can lead to both racial and gender-based discrimination.

The intersectionality of race and gender is also evident in issues such as reproductive rights and healthcare. Women of color often face barriers to accessing reproductive healthcare services due to systemic racism and sexism. They may experience higher rates of maternal mortality, limited access to contraception, and racial disparities in healthcare outcomes.

It is crucial to center the experiences of women of color in feminist discourse to ensure that their unique challenges are acknowledged and addressed. Intersectional feminism recognizes that the experiences of women are not universal, and it calls for a more inclusive approach that takes into account the intersecting identities of individuals.

The Intersectionality of LGBTQ+ Identity: Understanding the Unique Challenges Faced by Queer People of Color

Intersectionality is particularly relevant when examining the experiences of queer people of color. LGBTQ+ individuals already face discrimination and marginalization based on their sexual orientation or gender identity. However, when these identities intersect with race or ethnicity, they may face additional challenges.

For example, queer people of color may experience racism within LGBTQ+ communities or homophobia within their racial or ethnic communities. They may also face unique barriers to accessing healthcare, housing, and employment due to the intersection of their LGBTQ+ identity and their race or ethnicity.

Inclusivity is crucial in LGBTQ+ activism to ensure that the experiences of queer people of color are not overlooked or marginalized. Intersectional feminism recognizes the importance of addressing the intersecting identities of individuals and advocating for the rights and well-being of all marginalized communities.

The Intersectionality of Disability and Gender: Exploring the Complexities of Ableism and Sexism

The intersectionality of disability and gender highlights the unique challenges faced by disabled women. Disabled women often face both ableism and sexism, which can compound their experiences of discrimination and marginalization. They may face barriers to accessing education, employment, healthcare, and other essential services due to both their disability and their gender.

For example, disabled women may experience limited access to reproductive healthcare or face discrimination in the workplace due to ableist assumptions about their capabilities. They may also face higher rates of domestic violence or sexual assault, as they may be seen as more vulnerable or less able to defend themselves.

It is essential to prioritize disability rights within feminist discourse to ensure that the experiences of disabled women are acknowledged and addressed. Intersectional feminism recognizes that individuals hold multiple identities, and it calls for a more inclusive approach that takes into account the intersecting forms of oppression they face.

The Intersectionality of Class and Race: Examining the Interplay Between Economic and Racial Inequality

The intersectionality of class and race highlights the interplay between economic and racial inequality. Individuals who belong to marginalized racial or ethnic groups often face higher rates of poverty, limited access to education and employment opportunities, and systemic barriers to economic mobility.

For example, Black women may face both racial discrimination and gender-based wage gaps, which can contribute to higher rates of poverty and economic insecurity. They may also face limited access to affordable housing, healthcare, and other essential resources due to systemic racism and classism.

Addressing economic justice is crucial within feminist discourse to ensure that the experiences of marginalized women are acknowledged and addressed. Intersectional feminism recognizes that social issues cannot be understood or addressed in isolation from one another, and it calls for a more inclusive approach that takes into account the intersecting forms of oppression individuals face.

The Intersectionality of Religion and Gender: Understanding How Faith and Gender Identity Intersect

The intersectionality of religion and gender highlights the ways in which faith and gender identity intersect and shape individuals' experiences. Religious beliefs and practices can have a significant impact on gender roles, expectations, and opportunities within a community or society.

For example, some religious traditions may enforce strict gender norms or limit the leadership roles available to women. This can contribute to the marginalization and exclusion of women within religious spaces. Additionally, LGBTQ+ individuals may face discrimination or rejection from their religious communities due to their sexual orientation or gender identity.

Inclusivity is crucial within religious spaces to ensure that the experiences of marginalized individuals are acknowledged and respected.

Intersectional feminism recognizes the importance of addressing the intersecting identities of individuals and advocating for inclusivity and equality within all spheres of life.

The Intersectionality of Age and Gender: Exploring How Ageism and Sexism Affect Women

The intersectionality of age and gender highlights the unique challenges faced by older women. Older women often face both ageism and sexism, which can compound their experiences of discrimination and marginalization. They may face limited access to healthcare, employment opportunities, or social support due to both their age and their gender.

For example, older women may experience age-based stereotypes that portray them as less competent or less valuable in the workplace. They may also face limited representation in media or cultural narratives, which can contribute to their invisibility or marginalization.

Valuing the experiences of older women is crucial within feminist discourse to ensure that their unique challenges are acknowledged and addressed. Intersectional feminism recognizes that individuals hold multiple identities, and it calls for a more inclusive approach that takes into account the intersecting forms of oppression they face.

The Intersectionality of Nationality and Gender: Examining the Experiences of Immigrant Women

The intersectionality of nationality and gender highlights the unique challenges faced by immigrant women. Immigrant women often face both gender-based discrimination and xenophobia or racism, which can compound their experiences of marginalization and exclusion.

For example, immigrant women may face limited access to education, employment opportunities, or social support due to language barriers, cultural differences, or immigration policies. They may also face higher rates of domestic violence or exploitation due to their vulnerable immigration status.

Inclusivity is crucial in immigrant rights activism to ensure that the experiences of immigrant women are not overlooked or marginalized. Intersectional feminism recognizes the importance of addressing the intersecting identities of individuals and advocating for the rights and well-being of all marginalized communities.

The Intersectionality of Body Size and Gender: Understanding How Fatphobia and Sexism Intersect

The intersectionality of body size and gender highlights the ways in which fatphobia and sexism intersect to shape individuals' experiences. Society often places unrealistic beauty standards on women, which can contribute to body shaming, discrimination, and marginalization.

For example, fat women may face both weight-based discrimination and gender-based discrimination, which can compound their experiences of marginalization. They may face limited access to healthcare, employment opportunities, or social acceptance due to societal biases against larger bodies.

Promoting body positivity is crucial within feminist discourse to ensure that the experiences of individuals with diverse body sizes are acknowledged and respected. Intersectional feminism recognizes the importance of addressing the intersecting forms of oppression individuals face and advocating for inclusivity and equality for all.

The Importance of Intersectional Feminism: Why We Need to Center the Experiences of Marginalized Women

Intersectional feminism is crucial for creating a more inclusive and equitable society. By recognizing the interconnected nature of social categorizations, intersectionality allows for a more nuanced understanding of power dynamics and social inequality. It highlights the ways in which different forms of oppression reinforce and perpetuate one another, and it calls for a more inclusive approach to activism and social justice.

Centering the experiences of marginalized women is essential within feminist discourse to ensure that their unique challenges are acknowledged and addressed. Intersectional feminism recognizes that the experiences of women are not universal, and it calls for a more inclusive approach that takes into account the intersecting identities of individuals.

It is important to recognize that not all women experience oppression in the same way. Women of color, LGBTQ+ women, disabled women, older women, immigrant women, and women from different socioeconomic backgrounds all face unique challenges that must be addressed. By centering the experiences of marginalized women, intersectional feminism seeks to create a more inclusive and equitable society for all.

Intersectionality is a crucial framework for understanding the complexities of power dynamics and social inequality. It recognizes that individuals hold multiple identities and that these identities cannot be separated or understood in isolation from one another. By acknowledging the intersecting forms of oppression individuals face, intersectional feminism calls for a more inclusive approach to activism and social justice.

It is essential to center the experiences of marginalized women within feminist discourse to ensure that their unique challenges are acknowledged and addressed. Intersectional feminism recognizes that the experiences of women are not universal, and it calls for a more inclusive approach that takes into account the intersecting identities of individuals.

By embracing intersectionality, we can work towards creating a more inclusive and equitable society where all individuals are valued and respected. It is through this intersectional lens that we can truly understand and address the complexities of social inequality and work towards a more just and equal world.

Chapter 3: Living with Dual Diagnosis: One Person's Journey to Recovery

Dual diagnosis refers to the co-occurrence of a mental health disorder and substance abuse issue in an individual. This complex condition can have a significant impact on a person's life, affecting their daily functioning, relationships, and overall well-being. It is important to discuss and address dual diagnosis to ensure that individuals receive the support and treatment they need to recover and thrive.

What is Dual Diagnosis and How Does it Affect Your Life?

Dual diagnosis occurs when an individual experiences both a mental health disorder and a substance abuse issue simultaneously. Common mental health disorders that are often seen in conjunction with substance abuse include depression, anxiety disorders, bipolar disorder, and post-traumatic stress disorder (PTSD). Substance abuse can involve the misuse of drugs or alcohol.

The presence of both a mental health disorder and substance abuse issue can have a profound impact on an individual's life. It can make it difficult for them to maintain stable relationships, hold down a job, or engage in daily activities. The symptoms of the mental health disorder can be exacerbated by substance abuse, leading to increased distress and impairment in functioning.

The Stigma Surrounding Mental Illness and Substance Abuse

Societal stigma surrounding mental illness and addiction can be a significant barrier to individuals seeking help for dual diagnosis. There is often a lack of understanding and empathy towards those who are struggling with these conditions, leading to judgment and discrimination. This stigma can prevent individuals from reaching out for support and treatment, as they may fear being labeled or judged by others.

Breaking down the stigma surrounding mental illness and addiction is crucial in order to create an environment where individuals feel safe and supported in seeking help. Education and awareness campaigns can help to dispel myths and misconceptions about these conditions, promoting understanding and empathy. It is important for society as a whole to recognize that mental illness and addiction are medical conditions that require treatment, rather than moral failings or character flaws.

The Importance of Seeking Professional Help

Seeking professional help is essential for individuals with dual diagnosis to receive the support and treatment they need. Mental health professionals, such as psychiatrists, psychologists, and therapists, can provide a comprehensive assessment and diagnosis, as well as develop a personalized treatment plan. Substance abuse counselors and addiction specialists can offer guidance and support in overcoming addiction.

There are often barriers to seeking help for dual diagnosis, such as financial constraints, lack of access to healthcare services, and fear of judgment or stigma. It is important for individuals to overcome these barriers and reach out for support. There are resources available, such as community mental health centers, support groups, and helplines, that can provide assistance and guidance in finding appropriate treatment options.

Finding the Right Treatment Plan for Your Needs

There are various treatment options available for individuals with dual diagnosis, and it is important to find the right plan that meets their specific needs. Treatment may involve a combination of medication, therapy, support groups, and lifestyle changes. An individualized treatment plan takes into account the unique circumstances and challenges faced by each person.

Factors to consider when choosing a treatment plan include the severity of the mental health disorder and substance abuse issue, the individual's preferences and goals, and the availability of resources. It is important to work closely with healthcare professionals to develop a plan that addresses both the mental health disorder and substance abuse issue effectively.

The Role of Medication in Dual Diagnosis Recovery

Medication can play a crucial role in the recovery process for individuals with dual diagnosis. Medications may be prescribed to manage symptoms of the mental health disorder, such as antidepressants or mood stabilizers. In some cases, medications may also be used to assist with substance abuse recovery, such as medications that reduce cravings or block the effects of certain substances.

It is important to work closely with a healthcare provider when considering medication options for dual diagnosis. They can provide guidance on the benefits and potential drawbacks of different medications, as well as monitor their effectiveness and adjust dosages as needed. Medication should always be used in conjunction with therapy and other forms of treatment.

The Power of Therapy: Overcoming Trauma and Building Resilience

Therapy is a vital component of dual diagnosis recovery, as it can help individuals overcome trauma, build resilience, and develop healthy coping strategies. There are various therapy options available, including cognitive-behavioral therapy (CBT), dialectical behavior therapy (DBT), and trauma-focused therapy. These therapies can help individuals identify and challenge negative thought patterns, develop healthy coping skills, and process past traumas.

Finding the right therapist and therapy approach is important in order to ensure that individuals receive the support and guidance they need. It may be necessary to try different therapists or therapy modalities before finding the right fit. It is important for individuals to feel comfortable and supported in their therapeutic relationship.

Self-Care Strategies for Managing Mental Health and Addiction

Self-care is an essential aspect of dual diagnosis recovery, as it helps individuals manage their mental health and addiction on a daily basis. Self-care involves engaging in activities that promote physical, emotional, and mental well-being. Examples of self-care strategies include exercise, practicing mindfulness or meditation, engaging in hobbies or creative outlets, and maintaining a healthy diet.

Incorporating self-care into daily life can be challenging, especially when dealing with the symptoms of a mental health disorder or the cravings associated with addiction. However, making self-care a priority can have a significant impact on overall well-being and recovery. It is important for individuals to find activities that they enjoy and that provide them with a sense of fulfillment.

Navigating Relationships and Support Systems During Recovery

Having a strong support system is crucial in dual diagnosis recovery. Navigating relationships with family, friends, and coworkers can be challenging, as these individuals may not fully understand or be supportive of the recovery process. It is important for individuals to communicate their needs and boundaries clearly, and to seek out support from those who are understanding and empathetic.

Building a strong support system may involve reaching out to support groups or community organizations that specialize in dual diagnosis. These groups can provide a safe and supportive environment where individuals can share their experiences, receive guidance, and connect with others who are going through similar challenges.

Coping with Relapse and Building a Strong Relapse Prevention Plan

Relapse is a common occurrence in dual diagnosis recovery, and it is important for individuals to have a strong relapse prevention plan in place. Relapse should be viewed as a setback rather than a failure, and individuals should be prepared to seek help and support if it occurs. Coping strategies for managing relapse include reaching out to support systems, attending therapy or support group meetings, and engaging in self-care activities.

Building a strong relapse prevention plan involves identifying triggers and developing strategies to manage them effectively. It may involve making lifestyle changes, such as avoiding certain people or situations that may lead to substance abuse. It is important for individuals to be proactive in their recovery and take steps to prevent relapse.

The Journey to Long-Term Recovery: Celebrating Milestones and Setting Goals

The journey to long-term recovery is a process that requires dedication, perseverance, and support. It is important for individuals to celebrate milestones along the way, no matter how small they may seem. Celebrating milestones can provide motivation and encouragement to continue on the path of recovery.

Setting goals is also an important aspect of long-term recovery. Goals can provide direction and purpose, and help individuals stay focused on their recovery journey. Goals may include achieving abstinence from substances, improving mental health symptoms, or rebuilding relationships. It is important for individuals to set realistic and achievable goals, and to break them down into smaller, manageable steps.

Advocating for Yourself and Others: Breaking Down Barriers to Dual Diagnosis Treatment

There are often barriers to dual diagnosis treatment, such as lack of access to healthcare services, financial constraints, and stigma. It is important for individuals to advocate for themselves and others in accessing treatment. This may involve reaching out to healthcare providers, community organizations, or policymakers to voice concerns and advocate for change.

Breaking down barriers to treatment is crucial in order to ensure that all individuals have access to the support and resources they need. This may involve advocating for increased funding for mental health and addiction services, promoting education and awareness campaigns, and challenging societal attitudes towards mental illness and addiction.

Dual diagnosis is a complex condition that requires comprehensive support and treatment. It is important for individuals with dual diagnosis to seek professional help, develop an individualized treatment plan, and engage in self-care strategies. Navigating relationships and building a strong support system is crucial in the recovery process. Celebrating milestones and setting goals can provide motivation and direction. By advocating for themselves and others, individuals can help break down barriers to dual diagnosis treatment and promote understanding and empathy in society.

Chapter 4: From Shame to Empowerment: Overcoming Intrusive Thoughts

Intrusive thoughts are unwanted, distressing, and often disturbing thoughts or images that pop into our minds without our control. They can range from fleeting and harmless to persistent and distressing. Intrusive thoughts are a common experience for many people, but for some, they can have a significant impact on mental health. These thoughts can cause anxiety, depression, and even lead to self-blame and isolation. Understanding the power of intrusive thoughts and learning how to manage them is crucial for maintaining good mental health.

The Power of Intrusive Thoughts: Understanding Their Impact on Mental Health

Intrusive thoughts have the power to affect our mental health in various ways. They can create a constant state of anxiety and fear, as individuals may worry about the implications of these thoughts or fear that they will act on them. This constant worry can lead to heightened stress levels and difficulty in focusing on daily tasks. Intrusive thoughts can also contribute to feelings of depression, as individuals may feel overwhelmed by the negative content of these thoughts.

Common examples of intrusive thoughts include violent or aggressive thoughts towards oneself or others, sexual thoughts that are unwanted or inappropriate, and thoughts related to contamination or germs. These thoughts can be distressing and cause individuals to question their own morality or sanity. It is important to remember that having intrusive thoughts does not mean that a person wants to act on them or that they reflect their true desires or beliefs.

The Shame Spiral: How Intrusive Thoughts Can Lead to Self-Blame and Isolation

One of the most challenging aspects of intrusive thoughts is the shame and self-blame that often accompanies them. Individuals may feel guilty for having these thoughts, believing that they are a reflection of their character or morality. This shame can lead to a spiral of negative self-talk and self-blame, further exacerbating the impact of intrusive thoughts on mental health.

The shame associated with intrusive thoughts can also lead to isolation. Individuals may feel too embarrassed or ashamed to talk about their thoughts with others, fearing judgment or misunderstanding. This isolation can further worsen mental health, as individuals may avoid social situations or withdraw from relationships to protect themselves from potential judgment or rejection.

Breaking the Silence: Why Talking About Intrusive Thoughts is Crucial for Recovery

Breaking the silence and talking about intrusive thoughts is crucial for recovery. It is important to remember that intrusive thoughts are a common experience and that many people have them. By sharing our experiences with a therapist or trusted individual, we can reduce the shame and isolation associated with these thoughts.

Talking about intrusive thoughts can help individuals realize that they are not alone and that their experiences are valid. It can also provide an opportunity for education and understanding, as therapists or trusted individuals can provide information about the nature of intrusive thoughts and help individuals develop coping strategies.

Identifying Triggers: How to Recognize What Causes Intrusive Thoughts

Identifying triggers for intrusive thoughts is an important step in managing them. Triggers are situations, events, or thoughts that can activate or intensify intrusive thoughts. By recognizing these triggers, individuals can develop strategies to minimize their impact on mental health.

Common triggers for intrusive thoughts include stress, fatigue, trauma, and certain environments or situations that remind individuals of past traumatic experiences. It is important to pay attention to patterns and notice when intrusive thoughts tend to occur more frequently or intensely. This awareness can help individuals anticipate and prepare for potential triggers.

Cognitive Behavioral Therapy: A Proven Approach for Managing Intrusive Thoughts

Cognitive Behavioral Therapy (CBT) is a proven approach for managing intrusive thoughts. CBT focuses on identifying and challenging negative thought patterns and replacing them with more positive and realistic ones. It helps individuals develop coping strategies and skills to manage their thoughts and emotions effectively.

In the context of managing intrusive thoughts, CBT techniques may include cognitive restructuring, which involves identifying and challenging negative thought patterns, and exposure and response prevention, which involves gradually exposing oneself to the feared thoughts or situations and resisting the urge to engage in compulsive behaviors or rituals.

Mindfulness and Meditation: Techniques for Reducing the Intensity of Intrusive Thoughts

Mindfulness and meditation techniques can be helpful in reducing the intensity of intrusive thoughts. Mindfulness involves paying attention to the present moment without judgment, while meditation involves focusing one's attention on a specific object or activity. These practices can help individuals develop a greater sense of awareness and acceptance of their thoughts and emotions.

In the context of managing intrusive thoughts, mindfulness and meditation can help individuals observe their thoughts without getting caught up in them. By practicing non-judgmental awareness, individuals can learn to let go of intrusive thoughts and reduce their impact on mental health.

Medication: When and How to Use it for Intrusive Thoughts

In some cases, medication may be necessary for managing intrusive thoughts. Medications such as selective serotonin reuptake inhibitors

(SSRIs) or serotonin-norepinephrine reuptake inhibitors (SNRIs) may be prescribed to help regulate brain chemistry and reduce the frequency and intensity of intrusive thoughts.

It is important to consult with a healthcare professional to determine if medication is appropriate and to discuss potential side effects or interactions. Medication should always be used in conjunction with therapy or other forms of treatment for optimal results.

The Role of Self-Care: How Taking Care of Yourself Can Help Manage Intrusive Thoughts

Self-care plays a crucial role in managing intrusive thoughts. Taking care of oneself physically, emotionally, and mentally can help reduce stress levels and improve overall well-being. Engaging in activities that bring joy, practicing relaxation techniques, getting enough sleep, eating a balanced diet, and exercising regularly are all important aspects of self-care.

Self-care also involves setting boundaries and prioritizing one's needs. It is important to recognize when to take a break, say no to additional responsibilities, or seek support from others. By prioritizing self-care, individuals can better manage intrusive thoughts and maintain good mental health.

Finding Support: The Importance of Building a Support System for Recovery

Building a support system is crucial for managing intrusive thoughts. Having a network of supportive individuals who can provide understanding, empathy, and encouragement can make a significant difference in recovery. This support system can include friends, family members, therapists, support groups, or online communities.

It is important to reach out and ask for help when needed. Sharing experiences with others who have similar struggles can provide validation and a sense of belonging. Building a support system can also provide opportunities for learning from others' experiences and gaining new perspectives on managing intrusive thoughts.

Embracing Imperfection: How to Challenge the Need for Perfectionism in Managing Intrusive Thoughts

Perfectionism can exacerbate intrusive thoughts and make them more difficult to manage. The need for perfectionism can create unrealistic expectations and increase self-criticism. Challenging perfectionism involves recognizing that nobody is perfect and that it is okay to make mistakes or have intrusive thoughts.

Practicing self-compassion and self-acceptance is essential in challenging perfectionism. It involves treating oneself with kindness and understanding, acknowledging that intrusive thoughts are a normal part of the human experience, and reframing negative self-talk into more positive and realistic statements.

Moving Forward: Overcoming Intrusive Thoughts and Living a Fulfilling Life

Overcoming intrusive thoughts is possible with the right support and strategies in place. It is important to seek help from a therapist or trusted individual who can provide guidance and support throughout the recovery process. With time and practice, individuals can learn to manage their intrusive thoughts effectively and live a fulfilling life.

Managing intrusive thoughts does not mean that they will completely disappear, but rather that individuals can develop the skills and strategies to minimize their impact on mental health. It is important to remember that recovery is a journey, and setbacks may occur. However, with perseverance and support, individuals can continue moving forward and live a fulfilling life.

Intrusive thoughts can have a significant impact on mental health, but with the right strategies and support, they can be managed effectively. It is important to break the silence and talk about intrusive thoughts with a therapist or trusted individual to reduce shame and isolation. Identifying triggers, practicing cognitive behavioral therapy techniques, engaging in mindfulness and meditation, considering medication when necessary, prioritizing self-care, building a support system, challenging perfectionism, and seeking help are all important steps in managing intrusive thoughts. With time and practice, individuals can overcome intrusive thoughts and live a fulfilling life.

Chapter 5: Thriving in a Neurotypical World: Strategies for Navigating Social and Professional Settings

Neurotypicality and neurodiversity are terms that have gained recognition in recent years as society becomes more aware of the diverse range of neurological differences that exist among individuals. Neurotypicality refers to individuals who have typical neurological development and functioning, while neurodiversity encompasses the idea that neurological differences should be recognized and respected as a natural part of human diversity. Understanding and navigating neurotypical spaces is crucial for individuals who are neurodivergent, as it allows them to effectively communicate, build relationships, and thrive in various social settings.

Understanding Neurotypicality: What Does it Mean?

Neurotypicality refers to individuals who have typical neurological development and functioning. These individuals often possess certain characteristics that are considered "normal" or "typical" in society. They tend to have good social skills, easily understand nonverbal cues, and navigate social interactions with ease. Neurotypical individuals are often able to adapt to different social situations and understand the unwritten rules of social behavior.

The characteristics of neurotypical individuals can vary, but some common traits include good eye contact, strong verbal communication skills, and an ability to pick up on social cues such as body language and tone of voice. They may also have a natural ability to empathize with others and understand their emotions.

The Challenges of Navigating Neurotypical Spaces

For neurodivergent individuals, navigating neurotypical spaces can present a range of challenges. Neurotypical spaces refer to environments where the majority of individuals are neurotypical, such as workplaces, social events, and educational institutions. In these spaces, neurodivergent individuals may struggle to fit in or understand the unwritten rules of social behavior.

One common challenge faced by neurodivergent individuals in neurotypical spaces is difficulty with social interactions. They may struggle with understanding nonverbal cues or interpreting social situations, which can lead to misunderstandings or feelings of isolation. Additionally, neurodivergent individuals may find it challenging to navigate the social hierarchies and office politics that often exist in these spaces.

These challenges can have a significant impact on the mental health and well-being of neurodivergent individuals. They may experience increased levels of stress, anxiety, and depression as a result of feeling misunderstood or excluded. It is important for neurodivergent individuals to develop strategies for navigating these spaces and finding support networks that understand and appreciate their unique strengths and challenges.

Overcoming Social Anxiety: Tips and Tricks

Social anxiety is a common challenge faced by many neurodivergent individuals in neurotypical spaces. It refers to an intense fear or discomfort in social situations, which can make it difficult to engage in conversations, make friends, or participate in group activities. Social anxiety can be particularly challenging for neurodivergent individuals who may already struggle with social interactions.

There are several strategies that can help manage social anxiety. Deep breathing exercises can help calm the body and mind, reducing feelings of anxiety. Positive self-talk can also be effective in challenging negative thoughts and replacing them with more positive and realistic ones. It is important for neurodivergent individuals to remember that they are not alone in their struggles and that many others also experience social anxiety.

Building Strong Interpersonal Relationships

Building strong interpersonal relationships is important for both personal and professional success. In the workplace, strong relationships can lead to increased collaboration, productivity, and job satisfaction. In personal life, strong relationships provide support, companionship, and a sense of belonging.

For neurodivergent individuals, building strong relationships may require some additional effort and understanding. Active listening is a key skill that can help build strong relationships. This involves fully focusing on the speaker, maintaining eye contact, and responding appropriately to what is being said. Showing appreciation for others and their contributions can also help strengthen relationships. Taking the time to acknowledge and thank others for their efforts can go a long way in building trust and rapport.

The Power of Empathy in a Neurotypical World

Empathy is the ability to understand and share the feelings of others. It plays a crucial role in social interactions, allowing individuals to connect with and support one another. In a neurotypical world, empathy is particularly important for neurodivergent individuals who may struggle with social interactions.

Developing empathy skills can be beneficial for both neurotypical and neurodivergent individuals. It involves actively listening to others, trying to understand their perspective, and responding with kindness and compassion. Developing empathy skills can help bridge the gap between neurotypical and neurodivergent individuals, fostering understanding and acceptance.

Effective Communication Strategies for Success

Effective communication is essential for success in both personal and professional life. It involves clearly conveying messages, actively listening to others, and responding appropriately. In a neurotypical world, effective communication can be particularly challenging for neurodivergent individuals who may struggle with social cues or have difficulty expressing themselves.

There are several strategies that can help improve communication skills. Clear and concise messaging is important to ensure that the intended message is understood. Active listening involves fully focusing on the speaker, maintaining eye contact, and responding appropriately to what is being said. It is also important to be aware of nonverbal cues such as body language and tone of voice, as these can provide valuable information about how the message is being received.

Navigating Office Politics: Do's and Don'ts

Office politics refers to the complex dynamics and power struggles that exist within a workplace. It involves navigating relationships, managing conflicts, and understanding the unwritten rules of the office environment. Navigating office politics can be particularly challenging for neurodivergent individuals who may struggle with social interactions or have difficulty understanding social hierarchies.

There are several strategies that can help navigate office politics. Staying neutral and avoiding taking sides in conflicts can help maintain positive relationships with colleagues. Building alliances with trusted colleagues can also provide support and guidance in navigating office politics. It is important for neurodivergent individuals to be aware of the office politics dynamics and to seek support when needed.

Networking with Confidence: Tips for Introverts

Networking refers to the process of building professional relationships and connections. It is an important skill for career advancement and personal growth. However, networking can be particularly challenging for introverts, who may find large social gatherings or small talk draining or overwhelming.

There are several tips that can help introverts network with confidence. Setting goals before attending networking events can provide a sense of purpose and direction. Practicing self-care before and after networking events, such as taking breaks or engaging in activities that recharge introverts, can help manage energy levels. It is also important for introverts to remember that networking is about building genuine connections, not just collecting business cards.

The Importance of Self-Care in a High-Stress Environment

Self-care refers to activities and practices that promote physical, mental, and emotional well-being. In a high-stress environment, such as a neurotypical world, self-care becomes even more important for neurodivergent individuals who may be more susceptible to stress and burnout.

There are many different self-care practices that can be beneficial for neurodivergent individuals. Regular exercise can help reduce stress and improve overall well-being. Mindfulness practices, such as meditation or deep breathing exercises, can help calm the mind and promote relaxation. It is important for neurodivergent individuals to prioritize self-care and make time for activities that bring them joy and relaxation.

Balancing Work and Personal Life: Achieving Work-Life Balance

Work-life balance refers to the ability to effectively manage and prioritize both work and personal life. It is important for mental health and well-being, as it allows individuals to have time for relaxation, hobbies, and relationships outside of work. Achieving work-life balance can be particularly challenging in a neurotypical world where the demands of work can be overwhelming.

There are several tips that can help achieve work-life balance. Setting boundaries between work and personal life is crucial to ensure that time and energy are allocated to both areas. Prioritizing self-care and making time for activities that bring joy and relaxation is also important. It is important for neurodivergent individuals to remember that their well-being should be a priority and that it is okay to say no or ask for support when needed.

Embracing Neurodiversity: Celebrating Differences in the Workplace

Neurodiversity refers to the idea that neurological differences should be recognized and respected as a natural part of human diversity. Embracing neurodiversity in the workplace is important for creating an inclusive and supportive environment where all individuals can thrive.

There are many ways to embrace neurodiversity in the workplace. Providing accommodations, such as flexible work hours or quiet spaces, can help support neurodivergent individuals in their work. Offering diversity training and education can help raise awareness and understanding of neurodiversity among all employees. It is important for organizations to create a culture of acceptance and appreciation for neurodivergent individuals, recognizing their unique strengths and contributions.

Understanding and navigating neurotypical spaces is crucial for neurodivergent individuals to effectively communicate, build relationships, and thrive in various social settings. By developing strategies for managing social anxiety, building strong relationships, practicing empathy, and improving communication skills, neurodivergent individuals can navigate neurotypical spaces with confidence and success. Embracing neurodiversity in all aspects of life is important for creating a more inclusive and accepting society where all individuals can thrive.

Chapter 6: Challenging Stereotypes: How to Overcome Stigmas and Build Inclusive Communities

Stereotypes and stigmas are pervasive in society, shaping our perceptions and interactions with others. Stereotypes are generalized beliefs or assumptions about a particular group of people, often based on limited information or personal biases. Stigmas, on the other hand, are negative attitudes or beliefs that lead to the marginalization and discrimination of individuals or groups. Both stereotypes and stigmas can have harmful effects on individuals and communities, perpetuating inequality and hindering social progress.

Examples of stereotypes and stigmas can be found in various aspects of society. For instance, racial stereotypes have long been prevalent, perpetuating harmful beliefs about certain racial or ethnic groups. Gender stereotypes also persist, with women often being portrayed as emotional and nurturing, while men are expected to be strong and assertive. Additionally, individuals with mental health conditions often face stigmatization, leading to discrimination and barriers to accessing healthcare and employment opportunities.

The Harmful Effects of Stereotyping and Stigmatization

Stereotyping and stigmatization can have significant negative effects on individuals' mental health and well-being. When individuals are constantly subjected to negative stereotypes or stigmatized for their identities or characteristics, it can lead to feelings of shame, low self-esteem, and even depression or anxiety. The constant pressure to conform to societal expectations can be overwhelming and detrimental to one's mental health.

Moreover, stereotypes and stigmas limit opportunities and potential for individuals who are targeted by them. When people are judged based on preconceived notions rather than their individual abilities or qualifications, they may be denied job opportunities, educational opportunities, or equal treatment in various aspects of life. This not only hinders their personal growth but also perpetuates systemic inequalities.

Furthermore, stereotypes and stigmas contribute to discrimination and prejudice in society. When certain groups are consistently portrayed in a negative light or treated as inferior, it reinforces biases and prejudices, leading to discrimination and marginalization. This can manifest in various forms, such as racial profiling, hate crimes, or exclusion from social and economic opportunities. Stereotypes and stigmas perpetuate a cycle of discrimination that is difficult to break without conscious efforts to challenge and dismantle them.

Identifying Stereotypes and Stigmas in Society

Recognizing common stereotypes and stigmas is an essential step in challenging and dismantling them. It is important to be aware of the ways in which stereotypes and stigmas are perpetuated in society, as they often go unnoticed or are normalized. By identifying these harmful beliefs and attitudes, we can begin to understand their origins and work towards creating a more inclusive and accepting society.

Stereotypes and stigmas often originate from societal norms, cultural biases, or historical prejudices. They are perpetuated through media representation, education systems, and interpersonal interactions. For example, racial stereotypes may stem from historical prejudices and discriminatory practices that have been ingrained in society for generations. Similarly, gender stereotypes are often reinforced through media portrayals of traditional gender roles.

Understanding the origins of stereotypes and stigmas can help us challenge them more effectively. By questioning the validity of these beliefs and examining the evidence behind them, we can begin to dismantle the harmful narratives that perpetuate inequality and discrimination.

The Importance of Challenging Stereotypes and Stigmas

Challenging stereotypes and stigmas is crucial for creating a more inclusive and accepting society. By actively working to challenge these harmful beliefs and attitudes, we can promote diversity, understanding, empathy, and compassion.

Creating a more inclusive society means recognizing the value of diversity in all its forms. When we challenge stereotypes and stigmas, we open ourselves up to different perspectives, experiences, and ideas. This fosters a sense of belonging for individuals who have been marginalized or excluded based on stereotypes or stigmas.

Promoting diversity and understanding also leads to increased empathy and compassion. When we challenge stereotypes and stigmas, we are more likely to see individuals as unique human beings rather than as representatives of a particular group. This allows us to connect on a deeper level and build meaningful relationships based on mutual respect and understanding.

Strategies for Overcoming Stereotypes and Stigmas

There are several strategies that can be employed to overcome stereotypes and stigmas in society. Education and awareness-raising are essential tools in challenging these harmful beliefs and attitudes. By providing accurate information, promoting critical thinking, and encouraging open dialogue, we can help individuals recognize the harmful effects of stereotypes and stigmas.

Promoting positive representation and diversity in media, literature, and other forms of cultural expression is another effective strategy. By showcasing diverse perspectives and challenging traditional narratives, we can counteract the harmful stereotypes that have been perpetuated for so long. This includes providing platforms for marginalized voices to be heard and amplifying their stories and experiences.

Encouraging dialogue and open-mindedness is also crucial in challenging stereotypes and stigmas. By creating safe spaces for individuals to share their experiences and perspectives, we can foster understanding and empathy. This requires active listening, empathy, and a willingness to challenge our own biases and preconceived notions.

Building Inclusive Communities: Why It Matters

Building inclusive communities is essential for creating a society that values diversity, promotes equality, and fosters collaboration and innovation. Inclusive communities provide a sense of belonging and acceptance for all individuals, regardless of their identities or characteristics.

When individuals feel included and accepted in their communities, they are more likely to thrive personally, academically, and professionally. Inclusive communities provide opportunities for individuals to contribute their unique skills, talents, and perspectives, leading to increased collaboration and innovation.

Inclusive communities also promote social cohesion and harmony. When individuals from diverse backgrounds come together and interact on an equal footing, it breaks down barriers and fosters understanding and empathy. This leads to stronger social connections, increased trust, and a more cohesive society.

The Role of Education in Challenging Stereotypes and Stigmas

Education plays a crucial role in challenging stereotypes and stigmas. By incorporating diversity and inclusion into the curriculum, educators can help students develop a more nuanced understanding of the world and challenge their own biases.

Incorporating diverse perspectives and experiences into the curriculum allows students to see the world from different angles and challenge their preconceived notions. It also provides opportunities for students to learn about the contributions of marginalized groups throughout history and in contemporary society.

Encouraging critical thinking and questioning of stereotypes is another important aspect of education. By teaching students to question the validity of stereotypes and examine the evidence behind them, educators can help them develop a more nuanced understanding of individuals and communities.

Providing resources and support for marginalized groups is also crucial in education. This includes creating safe spaces for students to share their experiences, providing mentorship programs, and offering resources that promote diversity and inclusion.

Empowering Marginalized Groups to Challenge Stereotypes and Stigmas

Empowering marginalized groups to challenge stereotypes and stigmas is essential for creating a more inclusive society. By amplifying marginalized voices and perspectives, we can challenge the dominant narratives that perpetuate inequality and discrimination.

Providing platforms for advocacy and activism is one way to empower marginalized groups. By creating spaces for individuals to share their stories, raise awareness about their experiences, and advocate for change, we can amplify their voices and create meaningful social change.

Encouraging self-acceptance and empowerment is also crucial. By promoting self-confidence, self-esteem, and self-advocacy among marginalized individuals, we can help them challenge the stereotypes and stigmas that have been imposed upon them.

The Power of Media in Shaping Perceptions and Challenging Stereotypes

Media plays a powerful role in shaping perceptions and challenging stereotypes. By examining media representation and bias, we can better understand how stereotypes and stigmas are perpetuated and work towards promoting diverse representation.

Media has the power to shape public opinion and influence societal norms. When certain groups are consistently portrayed in a negative light or excluded from mainstream media, it reinforces biases and perpetuates stereotypes. By promoting diverse representation in media, we can challenge these harmful narratives and promote understanding and empathy.

Encouraging media literacy and critical consumption is also crucial. By teaching individuals to question the messages they receive from media and examine the underlying biases, we can empower them to challenge stereotypes and stigmas.

Overcoming Personal Biases to Build Inclusive Communities

Overcoming personal biases is essential for building inclusive communities. Recognizing and addressing our own biases is the first step towards creating a more inclusive society.

Self-reflection and growth are important aspects of overcoming personal biases. By examining our own beliefs, attitudes, and behaviors, we can identify areas where we may hold biases or perpetuate stereotypes. This requires humility, open-mindedness, and a willingness to learn from others.

Promoting empathy and understanding is also crucial in overcoming personal biases. By putting ourselves in others' shoes and seeking to understand their experiences, we can challenge our own preconceived notions and develop a more empathetic worldview.

Moving Towards a More Inclusive and Accepting Society

In conclusion, stereotypes and stigmas have harmful effects on individuals and communities, perpetuating inequality and hindering social progress. Challenging these harmful beliefs and attitudes is crucial for creating a more inclusive and accepting society.

By recognizing common stereotypes and stigmas, understanding their origins, and actively working to challenge them, we can promote diversity, understanding, empathy, and compassion. Strategies such as education and awareness-raising, promoting positive representation and diversity, encouraging dialogue and open-mindedness, and empowering marginalized groups are essential in this process.

Building inclusive communities is important for creating a society that values diversity, promotes equality, and fosters collaboration and innovation. Education plays a crucial role in challenging stereotypes and stigmas, while media has the power to shape perceptions and challenge harmful narratives.

Overcoming personal biases is essential for building inclusive communities. By recognizing and addressing our own biases, promoting empathy and understanding, and challenging our preconceived notions, we can contribute to a more inclusive and accepting society.

In moving towards a more inclusive and accepting future, it is important for individuals to take action towards challenging stereotypes and stigmas. By actively working to dismantle these harmful beliefs and attitudes, we can create a society that values diversity, promotes equality, and fosters understanding and empathy.

Chapter 7: Finding Your Path to Wellness: The Role of Therapeutic Strategies in Self-Care

Self-care is a term that has gained popularity in recent years, but what does it really mean? Simply put, self-care refers to the intentional actions and practices that individuals engage in to promote their physical, mental, and emotional well-being. It involves taking care of oneself in a holistic manner, addressing all aspects of health and wellness.

Self-care is crucial in achieving overall wellness because it allows individuals to prioritize their own needs and take steps towards maintaining a balanced and healthy life. In today's fast-paced and demanding world, it is easy to neglect self-care and focus solely on external responsibilities. However, neglecting self-care can lead to burnout, stress, and a decline in overall well-being.

There are various therapeutic strategies that can be incorporated into a self-care routine to enhance wellness. These strategies are designed to promote self-awareness, reduce stress, improve coping skills, and enhance overall quality of life. Some common therapeutic strategies include cognitive behavioral therapy (CBT), mindfulness and meditation practices, art therapy, and physical exercise.

Understanding Therapeutic Strategies and Their Benefits for Self-Care

Therapeutic strategies refer to the techniques and approaches used in various therapeutic modalities to promote healing and well-being. These strategies are evidence-based and have been proven effective in addressing specific mental health concerns or promoting overall wellness.

One popular therapeutic strategy is cognitive behavioral therapy (CBT), which focuses on identifying and changing negative thought patterns and behaviors that contribute to distress. CBT helps individuals develop healthier coping mechanisms and improve their overall mental well-being. Another therapeutic strategy is mindfulness, which involves being fully present in the moment without judgment. Mindfulness practices such as meditation and deep breathing exercises can help reduce stress, improve focus, and enhance overall well-being.

Art therapy is another therapeutic strategy that utilizes creative expression as a means of promoting self-discovery and healing. Through various art forms such as painting, drawing, or sculpting, individuals can explore their emotions, gain insight into their experiences, and find new ways of expressing themselves. Art therapy can be particularly beneficial for individuals who struggle with verbal communication or have difficulty processing emotions.

Identifying Your Personal Wellness Goals and Needs

Identifying personal wellness goals and needs is an essential step in the self-care journey. It allows individuals to gain clarity on what areas of their life they would like to improve and what actions they need to take to achieve their desired state of well-being.

To identify personal wellness goals and needs, it is important to take the time for self-reflection and introspection. This can be done through journaling, meditation, or simply taking a quiet moment to reflect on one's thoughts and feelings. It is helpful to ask oneself questions such as "What areas of my life am I currently unhappy with?" or "What activities bring me joy and fulfillment?"

Examples of personal wellness goals and needs may include improving physical fitness, managing stress more effectively, cultivating healthier relationships, or finding a better work-life balance. By identifying these goals and needs, individuals can then create a plan of action to address them and prioritize self-care in their daily lives.

The Role of Mindfulness and Meditation in Self-Care

Mindfulness is the practice of intentionally focusing one's attention on the present moment without judgment. It involves being fully aware of one's thoughts, feelings, bodily sensations, and the surrounding environment. Meditation is a specific technique used to cultivate mindfulness.

Incorporating mindfulness and meditation into a self-care routine can have numerous benefits for overall well-being. Research has shown that regular mindfulness practice can reduce stress, improve sleep quality, enhance focus and attention, and increase overall feelings of well-being. It can also help individuals develop a greater sense of self-awareness and improve their ability to regulate emotions.

To incorporate mindfulness and meditation into a self-care routine, individuals can start by setting aside a few minutes each day to practice. This can be done through guided meditation apps, attending mindfulness classes or workshops, or simply finding a quiet space to sit and focus on one's breath. It is important to approach mindfulness and meditation with an open mind and be patient with oneself as it takes time to develop these skills.

How Cognitive Behavioral Therapy Can Help You Achieve Wellness

Cognitive behavioral therapy (CBT) is a therapeutic approach that focuses on the connection between thoughts, feelings, and behaviors. It aims to help individuals identify and change negative thought patterns and behaviors that contribute to distress.

CBT can be particularly beneficial for self-care as it provides individuals with practical tools and strategies to manage stress, improve coping skills, and enhance overall well-being. Through CBT, individuals learn to challenge negative thoughts and replace them with more positive and realistic ones. They also learn effective problem-solving skills and develop healthier ways of coping with difficult emotions.

For example, if an individual is struggling with anxiety, CBT can help them identify the underlying thoughts that contribute to their anxiety and challenge their validity. They can then learn techniques such as deep breathing exercises or progressive muscle relaxation to manage their anxiety symptoms. CBT can also help individuals develop healthier habits and routines that promote overall well-being, such as improving sleep hygiene or incorporating regular exercise into their daily lives.

The Benefits of Incorporating Yoga and Exercise into Your Self-Care Routine

Physical exercise is an essential component of self-care as it has numerous benefits for both physical and mental well-being. Regular exercise can improve cardiovascular health, strengthen muscles and bones, boost mood, reduce stress, and improve sleep quality.

Yoga, in particular, is a form of exercise that combines physical movement with mindfulness and breath awareness. It has been shown to have numerous benefits for overall well-being. Yoga can improve flexibility, strength, and balance, as well as promote relaxation and reduce stress. It can also help individuals develop a greater sense of body awareness and improve their ability to regulate emotions.

To incorporate yoga and exercise into a self-care routine, individuals can start by setting aside dedicated time each day or week for physical activity. This can be as simple as going for a walk, taking a yoga class, or following an online workout video. It is important to choose activities that are enjoyable and sustainable in the long term to ensure consistency and adherence.

Exploring the Benefits of Art Therapy for Self-Care and Wellness

Art therapy is a therapeutic approach that utilizes creative expression as a means of promoting self-discovery, healing, and overall well-being. It involves engaging in various art forms such as painting, drawing, or sculpting under the guidance of a trained art therapist.

Art therapy can be particularly beneficial for self-care as it provides individuals with a safe and non-judgmental space to explore their emotions, gain insight into their experiences, and find new ways of expressing themselves. Through the creative process, individuals can tap into their subconscious mind and access deeper levels of self-awareness.

The benefits of art therapy for self-care and wellness are numerous. It can help reduce stress, improve mood, enhance self-esteem, and promote relaxation. Art therapy can also provide individuals with a sense of empowerment and control over their own healing process.

To incorporate art therapy into a self-care routine, individuals can start by setting aside dedicated time each week for creative expression. This can be done through journaling, painting, drawing, or any other form of artistic expression that resonates with them. It is important to approach art therapy with an open mind and focus on the process rather than the end result.

The Role of Nutrition in Achieving Optimal Wellness

Nutrition plays a crucial role in achieving optimal wellness as it provides the body with the necessary nutrients to function properly. A balanced and nutritious diet can improve energy levels, support immune function, promote healthy digestion, and reduce the risk of chronic diseases.

To incorporate healthy eating habits into a self-care routine, individuals can start by focusing on whole, unprocessed foods such as fruits, vegetables, whole grains, lean proteins, and healthy fats. It is also important to stay hydrated by drinking an adequate amount of water throughout the day.

Meal planning and preparation can be helpful in ensuring that individuals have access to nutritious meals and snacks throughout the week. This can involve batch cooking, meal prepping, or simply making a grocery list and planning meals in advance.

How to Build a Support System to Enhance Your Self-Care Journey

Building a support system is essential in enhancing the self-care journey. It provides individuals with a network of people who can offer guidance, encouragement, and accountability.

To build a support system, it is important to identify individuals who are supportive and understanding of one's self-care goals and needs. This can include friends, family members, or even professionals such as therapists or coaches. It is important to communicate one's needs and boundaries with these individuals and seek their support when needed.

Support systems can also be built through joining support groups or engaging in online communities that focus on self-care and wellness. These groups provide individuals with a sense of belonging and allow them to connect with others who are on a similar journey.

Overcoming Barriers and Obstacles in Your Path to Wellness

There are common barriers and obstacles that individuals may face on their path to wellness. These can include time constraints, financial limitations, lack of motivation or support, or fear of change.

To overcome these barriers and obstacles, it is important to first identify them and acknowledge their presence. This can be done through self-reflection or seeking guidance from a therapist or coach. Once identified, individuals can then develop strategies to address these barriers and find alternative solutions.

For example, if time constraints are a barrier to engaging in self-care activities, individuals can explore ways to prioritize their time and create a schedule that allows for self-care. This may involve delegating tasks, setting boundaries, or reevaluating one's priorities.

It is also important to practice self-compassion and be patient with oneself when facing obstacles. Change takes time and effort, and setbacks are a normal part of the process. By approaching obstacles with a growth mindset and seeking support when needed, individuals can overcome barriers and continue on their path to wellness.

The Power of Therapeutic Strategies in Achieving a Balanced and Healthy Life

In conclusion, self-care is essential in achieving overall wellness. It involves prioritizing one's own needs and engaging in intentional actions and practices that promote physical, mental, and emotional well-being.

Therapeutic strategies such as cognitive behavioral therapy, mindfulness and meditation practices, art therapy, yoga, exercise, nutrition, and building a support system can all enhance the self-care journey. These strategies provide individuals with practical tools and techniques to manage stress, improve coping skills, enhance self-awareness, and promote overall well-being.

It is important to prioritize self-care and seek support when needed. By incorporating therapeutic strategies into a self-care routine and addressing barriers and obstacles along the way, individuals can achieve a balanced and healthy life. Remember that self-care is not selfish but rather an essential part of maintaining overall wellness.

Chapter 8: The Science Behind Emotional Regulation: How It Can Improve Your Life

Emotional regulation refers to the ability to manage and control one's emotions in a healthy and adaptive way. It involves recognizing and understanding our emotions, as well as being able to respond to them in a way that is appropriate and beneficial. Emotional regulation is an essential skill that plays a crucial role in our daily lives, impacting our mental health, relationships, and overall well-being.

The Role of the Brain in Emotional Regulation

The brain plays a significant role in emotional regulation. Two key areas of the brain involved in this process are the limbic system and the prefrontal cortex. The limbic system, which includes structures such as the amygdala and hippocampus, is responsible for processing emotions and generating emotional responses. It plays a crucial role in our fight-or-flight response and helps us recognize and react to potential threats.

On the other hand, the prefrontal cortex is responsible for executive functioning, which includes decision-making, impulse control, and emotional regulation. It helps us regulate our emotions by inhibiting or modulating the activity of the limbic system. When the prefrontal cortex is functioning properly, it can help us regulate our emotions effectively. However, when it is impaired or underdeveloped, emotional dysregulation can occur.

The Link Between Emotional Regulation and Mental Health

Emotional dysregulation can have a significant impact on mental health. When we struggle to regulate our emotions, it can lead to various mental health issues such as anxiety, depression, and mood disorders. For example, individuals who have difficulty managing their anger may experience frequent outbursts or engage in aggressive behavior, which can negatively affect their relationships and overall well-being.

On the other hand, practicing emotional regulation can have numerous benefits for mental health. It can help reduce symptoms of anxiety and depression, improve mood stability, and enhance overall emotional well-being. By learning to regulate our emotions, we can develop healthier coping mechanisms and improve our ability to handle stress and adversity.

How Emotional Regulation Can Improve Your Relationships

Emotional regulation plays a crucial role in our relationships. When we are able to regulate our emotions effectively, it can positively impact our communication and conflict resolution skills. By being aware of and managing our emotions, we can express ourselves more clearly and empathetically, leading to better understanding and connection with others.

On the other hand, when we struggle with emotional regulation, it can lead to difficulties in communication and conflict resolution. For example, if we are unable to control our anger, we may lash out at others or say hurtful things that can damage our relationships. By practicing emotional regulation, we can improve our ability to respond to conflicts in a calm and constructive manner, leading to healthier and more fulfilling relationships.

The Benefits of Practicing Emotional Regulation

Practicing emotional regulation has numerous benefits for our overall well-being. Firstly, it improves our emotional well-being by allowing us to experience a wider range of positive emotions and reducing the intensity and duration of negative emotions. By regulating our emotions, we can cultivate a greater sense of happiness, contentment, and fulfillment in our lives.

Additionally, emotional regulation increases resilience. When we are able to regulate our emotions effectively, we are better equipped to handle stress and adversity. We can bounce back more quickly from setbacks and maintain a positive outlook even in challenging situations. This resilience allows us to navigate life's ups and downs with greater ease and adaptability.

Furthermore, emotional regulation enhances decision-making. When we are in a heightened emotional state, it can cloud our judgment and lead to impulsive or irrational decisions. By regulating our emotions, we can approach decision-making with clarity and rationality, leading to better choices and outcomes.

Techniques for Improving Emotional Regulation

There are various techniques that can help improve emotional regulation. One effective technique is deep breathing exercises. Deep breathing activates the body's relaxation response and helps calm the nervous system. By taking slow, deep breaths, we can reduce feelings of stress and anxiety and promote a sense of calm and relaxation.

Another technique is cognitive restructuring. This involves identifying and challenging negative or irrational thoughts that contribute to emotional dysregulation. By replacing these thoughts with more positive and realistic ones, we can shift our perspective and regulate our emotions more effectively.

Mindfulness practices are also beneficial for improving emotional regulation. Mindfulness involves paying attention to the present moment without judgment. By practicing mindfulness, we can become more aware of our emotions and learn to observe them without getting caught up in them. This allows us to respond to our emotions in a more intentional and controlled manner.

Mindfulness and Emotional Regulation

Mindfulness plays a crucial role in emotional regulation. By cultivating a mindful awareness of our emotions, we can develop a greater understanding of them and respond to them in a more skillful way. Mindfulness helps us observe our emotions without judgment or reactivity, allowing us to regulate them more effectively.

There are various mindfulness techniques that can be used to improve emotional regulation. One technique is body scan meditation, where we systematically bring our attention to different parts of the body, noticing any sensations or emotions that arise. This practice helps us develop a greater awareness of our bodily sensations and emotions, allowing us to regulate them more effectively.

Another technique is loving-kindness meditation, where we cultivate feelings of love, compassion, and kindness towards ourselves and others. This practice helps us develop a positive and compassionate attitude towards our emotions, allowing us to regulate them with greater ease and acceptance.

The Importance of Self-Compassion in Emotional Regulation

Self-compassion is an essential component of emotional regulation. When we are self-critical or judgmental towards ourselves, it can exacerbate emotional dysregulation. On the other hand, practicing self-compassion involves treating ourselves with kindness, understanding, and acceptance, even in the face of difficult emotions.

By cultivating self-compassion, we can create a safe and supportive internal environment that allows us to regulate our emotions more effectively. When we approach our emotions with kindness and acceptance, we are more likely to respond to them in a healthy and adaptive way.

How Emotional Regulation Can Help You Achieve Your Goals

Emotional regulation plays a crucial role in goal achievement. When we are able to regulate our emotions effectively, we can stay focused and motivated towards our goals. By managing our emotions, we can overcome obstacles and setbacks with resilience and determination.

On the other hand, when we struggle with emotional dysregulation, it can hinder our progress towards our goals. For example, if we become overwhelmed by fear or self-doubt, it can prevent us from taking necessary risks or pursuing our dreams. By practicing emotional regulation, we can overcome these barriers and move closer towards achieving our goals.

Emotional Regulation and Stress Management

Emotional regulation is closely linked to stress management. When we are able to regulate our emotions effectively, it can help reduce stress levels and promote a sense of calm and relaxation. By managing our emotions, we can prevent them from escalating into chronic stress or anxiety.

There are various techniques that can be used to use emotional regulation for stress management. One technique is progressive muscle relaxation, where we systematically tense and relax different muscle groups in the body. This practice helps release tension and promotes a sense of relaxation.

Another technique is journaling, where we write down our thoughts and emotions as a way of processing and releasing them. By expressing our emotions on paper, we can gain clarity and perspective, reducing feelings of stress and overwhelm.

The Power of Emotional Regulation in Transforming Your Life

In conclusion, emotional regulation is a vital skill that has numerous benefits for our overall well-being. By learning to regulate our emotions effectively, we can improve our mental health, enhance our relationships, and achieve our goals. Through techniques such as deep breathing exercises, cognitive restructuring, and mindfulness practices, we can cultivate emotional regulation and transform our lives for the better. So, let us embrace the power of emotional regulation and embark on a journey towards greater emotional well-being and fulfillment.

Chapter 9: The Power of Communication in Strengthening Family Dynamics

Communication is a fundamental aspect of human interaction, and it plays a crucial role in building strong and healthy family relationships. Effective communication within a family unit fosters understanding, trust, and intimacy among its members. It allows family members to express their thoughts, feelings, and needs openly and honestly, creating an environment where everyone feels heard and valued. On the other hand, poor communication can lead to misunderstandings, conflicts, and strained relationships within the family. Therefore, it is essential to recognize the significance of communication in family dynamics and strive to improve it.

Understanding the role of communication in building trust and intimacy

Open and honest communication is the foundation of trust within a family. When family members communicate openly, they create an atmosphere of transparency and authenticity. This enables them to share their thoughts, concerns, and vulnerabilities without fear of judgment or rejection. As a result, trust is built, and family members feel safe and secure in expressing themselves.

Effective communication also enhances intimacy within family relationships. By openly sharing their thoughts and feelings, family members develop a deeper understanding of one another. This understanding fosters emotional connection and empathy, which are essential components of intimacy. When family members communicate effectively, they create a space where they can support each other emotionally and build stronger bonds.

Communication as a tool for conflict resolution and problem-solving

Conflict is inevitable in any relationship, including within families. However, effective communication can play a significant role in resolving conflicts and finding solutions to problems. When conflicts arise, open and honest communication allows family members to express their concerns and perspectives without resorting to aggression or hostility.

Effective communication strategies for conflict resolution include active listening, empathy, and compromise. Active listening involves giving full attention to the speaker, seeking clarification when needed, and responding with empathy. Empathy allows family members to understand each other's emotions and perspectives better, which can lead to finding common ground and resolving conflicts.

The impact of effective communication on children's emotional well-being

Communication within the family has a profound impact on children's emotional development and well-being. When parents communicate positively with their children, it helps them feel loved, valued, and understood. This, in turn, promotes their self-esteem and emotional resilience.

Positive communication involves actively listening to children, validating their feelings, and providing them with a safe space to express themselves. When children feel heard and understood, they are more likely to develop healthy emotional regulation skills and have better mental health outcomes.

On the other hand, poor communication within the family can have detrimental effects on children's emotional well-being. When children are not given the opportunity to express themselves or are met with criticism and judgment, they may develop low self-esteem, anxiety, or depression. Therefore, it is crucial for parents to prioritize positive communication with their children to promote their emotional well-being.

Overcoming communication barriers in multicultural families

In multicultural families, communication can present unique challenges due to language barriers, cultural differences, and varying communication styles. However, it is essential to overcome these barriers to foster understanding and connection within the family.

Strategies for overcoming communication barriers in multicultural families include learning each other's languages or using translation tools to facilitate communication. It is also important to be open-minded and respectful of different cultural norms and practices. By actively seeking to understand and appreciate each other's perspectives, multicultural families can bridge the communication gap and build stronger relationships.

The role of active listening and empathy in family communication

Active listening and empathy are crucial components of effective communication within the family. Active listening involves giving one's full attention to the speaker, maintaining eye contact, and providing verbal and non-verbal cues that show understanding and engagement.

Empathy goes hand in hand with active listening. It involves putting oneself in the other person's shoes and trying to understand their emotions and perspectives. By practicing empathy, family members can create a supportive and understanding environment where everyone feels valued and heard.

To practice active listening and empathy in family communication, it is important to be present in the moment, avoid distractions, and genuinely listen to what the other person is saying. It is also important to validate their feelings and respond with empathy rather than judgment or criticism.

Communication strategies for busy and stressed families

In today's fast-paced world, many families find themselves juggling multiple responsibilities and facing high levels of stress. This can make communication within the family challenging. However, there are strategies that busy and stressed families can employ to improve communication.

One effective strategy is to set aside dedicated time for family communication. This can be a daily or weekly ritual where family members come together to talk, share, and connect. It is important to create a safe and non-judgmental space where everyone feels comfortable expressing themselves.

Another strategy is to prioritize quality over quantity when it comes to communication. Even if time is limited, making the most of the time available by being fully present and engaged can make a significant difference. This means putting away distractions such as phones or laptops and giving one's full attention to the conversation.

The dangers of poor communication and how to avoid them

Poor communication within the family can have negative consequences on relationships and overall family dynamics. It can lead to misunderstandings, conflicts, resentment, and a breakdown in trust. Therefore, it is crucial to avoid poor communication habits and promote positive communication within the family.

One way to avoid poor communication is by being mindful of one's language and tone. Using respectful and non-confrontational language can prevent misunderstandings and defensiveness. It is also important to avoid making assumptions or jumping to conclusions without seeking clarification.

Another way to promote positive communication is by practicing active listening and empathy. By genuinely listening to each other and trying to understand each other's perspectives, family members can avoid miscommunication and build stronger connections.

The importance of setting boundaries and expectations in family communication

Setting healthy boundaries and expectations is essential for effective communication within the family. Boundaries help define what is acceptable and what is not in terms of communication, ensuring that everyone feels respected and safe.

Setting expectations also helps create a framework for communication within the family. This can include guidelines on how conflicts should be resolved, how emotions should be expressed, and how decisions should be made collectively.

By setting clear boundaries and expectations, family members can navigate communication more effectively and prevent misunderstandings or conflicts from arising.

How technology affects family communication and ways to use it effectively

Technology has become an integral part of our lives, including within family dynamics. While it can facilitate communication, it can also present challenges if not used effectively.

One way technology affects family communication is by creating distractions. The constant presence of smartphones or other devices can take away from quality face-to-face interactions. Therefore, it is important to set boundaries around technology use within the family, such as designated tech-free times or areas.

On the other hand, technology can also be used as a tool to enhance family communication. Video calls or messaging apps can help families stay connected even when physically apart. It is important to use technology mindfully and intentionally, ensuring that it serves as a means to strengthen relationships rather than replace them.

Emphasizing the importance of open and honest communication in family dynamics

In conclusion, open and honest communication is vital for building strong and healthy family relationships. It fosters trust, intimacy, and understanding among family members. Effective communication also plays a crucial role in conflict resolution, problem-solving, and promoting children's emotional well-being.

Overcoming communication barriers in multicultural families, practicing active listening and empathy, and setting boundaries and expectations are all strategies that can enhance communication within the family. It is also important to be mindful of the impact of technology on family communication and use it effectively.

By prioritizing open and honest communication, families can create a supportive and nurturing environment where everyone feels valued and heard. This, in turn, strengthens family bonds and promotes overall well-being.

Chapter 10: The Power of Expression: Giving Autistic Voices a Platform

Autism is a neurodevelopmental disorder that affects individuals in various ways. It is characterized by difficulties in social interaction, communication, and repetitive behaviors. However, it is important to recognize that autism is not a one-size-fits-all condition. Each autistic individual has their own unique experiences, perspectives, and voices that deserve to be heard and valued.

Listening to and valuing autistic voices is crucial for several reasons. First and foremost, it promotes inclusivity and diversity. By giving autistic individuals a platform to express themselves, we are acknowledging their worth and recognizing their contributions to society. Additionally, hearing from autistic voices can provide valuable insights and perspectives that can help us better understand the experiences of those on the autism spectrum. This understanding can lead to more effective support systems and accommodations for autistic individuals.

Breaking the Stereotypes: Dispelling Common Misconceptions about Autism

There are many stereotypes and misconceptions surrounding autism that can hinder our ability to truly understand and appreciate autistic voices. One common misconception is that all autistic individuals are nonverbal or have severe intellectual disabilities. While some autistic individuals may have difficulty with speech or have intellectual disabilities, this is not true for everyone on the spectrum. In fact, many autistic individuals are highly intelligent and have unique talents and abilities.

Another stereotype is that autistic individuals lack empathy or emotional connection with others. This is simply not true. Autistic individuals may experience empathy differently or struggle with expressing it in ways that are recognizable to neurotypical individuals, but they are capable of feeling deeply and forming meaningful connections with others.

Personal experiences from autistic individuals themselves can help dispel these stereotypes. Many autistic advocates have shared their stories and insights, challenging these misconceptions and providing a more accurate representation of what it means to be autistic.

The Power of Expression: How Autistic Voices Can Make a Difference

Autistic voices have the power to make a significant difference in society. By sharing their experiences and perspectives, autistic individuals can help raise awareness and understanding about autism. They can challenge societal norms and expectations, advocating for acceptance and inclusion.

There are numerous examples of autistic individuals who have made a difference through their voices. Temple Grandin, a renowned autism advocate, has used her platform to educate others about autism and promote understanding. She has written books, given TED talks, and consulted on the design of livestock handling facilities, using her unique perspective as an autistic individual to improve animal welfare.

Another example is Carly Fleischmann, a nonverbal autistic woman who communicates through typing. She has become an advocate for autism awareness and has her own talk show where she interviews celebrities and shares her experiences as an autistic individual.

These examples highlight the unique perspectives and insights that autistic voices can bring. By listening to and valuing these voices, we can gain a deeper understanding of autism and create a more inclusive society.

The Challenges of Communication: Insights into the Autistic Experience

Communication is one of the core challenges that many autistic individuals face. Difficulties with verbal and nonverbal communication can make it challenging for them to express themselves and be understood by others. This can lead to frustration, isolation, and misunderstandings.

It is important for society to recognize these communication challenges and make accommodations to support autistic individuals. This can include providing alternative forms of communication such as sign language or assistive technology devices. It also involves being patient, listening actively, and creating an environment that is conducive to effective communication.

By understanding the communication challenges that autistic individuals face, we can work towards creating a more inclusive society where their voices are heard and valued.

The Role of Technology: Empowering Autistic Voices through Assistive Devices

Technology plays a crucial role in empowering autistic voices. Assistive devices can provide alternative means of communication for those who struggle with verbal communication. These devices can range from simple picture-based communication boards to more advanced speech-generating devices.

Assistive technology not only helps autistic individuals express themselves, but it also enhances their independence and autonomy. It allows them to participate more fully in social interactions, education, and employment opportunities.

One example of assistive technology is the use of tablets and apps that provide visual supports and communication tools. These apps can help individuals with autism communicate their needs, preferences, and emotions. They can also assist with daily living skills, such as organizing schedules and managing tasks.

The benefits of assistive technology extend beyond communication. Virtual reality technology, for example, can be used to create immersive environments that help autistic individuals practice social skills in a safe and controlled setting.

By harnessing the power of technology, we can empower autistic individuals to express themselves and participate more fully in society.

The Importance of Advocacy: Creating Opportunities for Autistic Voices to be Heard

Advocacy plays a crucial role in ensuring that autistic voices are heard and valued. Autistic individuals often face barriers to inclusion and acceptance due to societal attitudes and misconceptions about autism. Advocacy efforts aim to challenge these barriers and create opportunities for autistic individuals to have their voices heard.

Advocacy can take many forms, from grassroots movements to policy changes at the national level. It involves raising awareness about autism, promoting acceptance and inclusion, and advocating for the rights and needs of autistic individuals.

Autistic self-advocacy is particularly important. Autistic individuals are the experts on their own experiences, and their voices should be at the forefront of any discussions or decisions that affect them. By amplifying autistic voices and giving them a platform to share their stories, we can create a more inclusive society that values diversity.

The Benefits of Inclusion: How Including Autistic Voices Can Benefit Society

Including autistic voices in society has numerous benefits for both autistic individuals and the broader community. First and foremost, it promotes diversity and fosters a more inclusive society. By valuing and including autistic individuals, we are recognizing their worth and contributions to society.

Autistic voices can also bring unique perspectives and insights that can help us solve complex problems and think outside the box. Many autistic individuals have exceptional attention to detail, pattern recognition skills, and the ability to think in a logical and systematic manner. These strengths can be valuable in fields such as science, technology, engineering, and mathematics.

Inclusion also promotes empathy and understanding. By hearing from autistic voices, we can gain a deeper understanding of their experiences and challenges. This understanding can lead to more compassionate and inclusive communities.

The Impact of Stigma: Addressing Negative Attitudes towards Autism and Autistic People

Stigma surrounding autism can have a significant negative impact on autistic individuals. It can lead to discrimination, exclusion, and a lack of opportunities. Negative attitudes towards autism can also perpetuate stereotypes and misconceptions, further marginalizing autistic voices.

Addressing and combating negative attitudes towards autism is crucial for creating a more inclusive society. Education plays a key role in challenging these attitudes. By providing accurate information about autism and promoting understanding, we can break down stereotypes and promote acceptance.

Media representation is another important factor in addressing stigma. By portraying autistic individuals in a positive and accurate light, media can help challenge negative attitudes and promote acceptance.

It is also important for society to recognize the strengths and talents of autistic individuals. By focusing on their abilities rather than their disabilities, we can create a more inclusive society that values diversity.

The Need for Understanding: Building Bridges between Autistic and Non-Autistic Communities

Building bridges between autistic and non-autistic communities is crucial for fostering understanding and acceptance. It is important for non-autistic individuals to educate themselves about autism and learn how to be allies to the autistic community.

Understanding and acceptance go hand in hand. By seeking to understand the experiences and perspectives of autistic individuals, we can create a more inclusive society that values diversity. This understanding can lead to more effective support systems and accommodations for autistic individuals.

Building bridges also involves creating opportunities for autistic and non-autistic individuals to interact and learn from each other. This can be done through community events, workshops, and support groups. By fostering these connections, we can break down barriers and promote inclusivity.

The Future of Autistic Expression: Exploring New Opportunities for Autistic Voices

The future holds great potential for new opportunities and platforms for autistic expression. As technology continues to advance, there are increasing possibilities for autistic individuals to share their voices and experiences.

Social media platforms have already provided a space for autistic individuals to connect with each other and share their stories. Autistic bloggers, vloggers, and podcasters have emerged as influential voices in the autism community, challenging stereotypes and promoting acceptance.

In addition to social media, there are also opportunities for autistic individuals to contribute to research, policy-making, and advocacy efforts. By involving autistic voices in these processes, we can ensure that decisions are made with their best interests in mind.

It is important to continue creating and expanding these opportunities for autistic expression. By doing so, we can celebrate the diversity of human experiences and promote a more inclusive society.

Celebrating Diversity and the Power of Expression

In conclusion, valuing and listening to autistic voices is crucial for creating a more inclusive society. Autistic individuals have unique perspectives, insights, and talents that deserve to be heard and valued. By breaking down stereotypes, addressing stigma, and fostering understanding, we can create a society that celebrates diversity and promotes inclusivity.

The power of expression is not limited to any one group of individuals. It is a fundamental human right that should be extended to all. By celebrating the diversity of human experiences and promoting the power of expression in all individuals, including those on the autism spectrum, we can create a more compassionate and inclusive world.

Don't miss out!

Visit the website below and you can sign up to receive emails whenever Travis Breeding publishes a new book. There's no charge and no obligation.

https://books2read.com/r/B-A-CBXDB-PKFXC

BOOKS 2 READ

Connecting independent readers to independent writers.

Did you love *Unraveling The Mind: Understanding OCD, Autism, And Obsession*? Then you should read *Celebrating Neurodiversity*[1] by Travis Breeding!

[2]

"Celebrating Neurodiversity" is not just a book; it's a manifesto for acceptance, understanding, and inclusivity. Breeding passionately advocates for the celebration of differences, urging readers to embrace the mosaic of neurodiversity that enriches our society. Through empowering stories of resilience, creativity, and innovation, Breeding showcases the immense potential that lies within the neurodivergent community.

From the unique ways in which neurodivergent individuals perceive the world to the invaluable insights they offer, "Celebrating Neurodiversity" is a thought-provoking exploration of what it truly

---

1. https://books2read.com/u/4DnjxP

2. https://books2read.com/u/4DnjxP

means to be neurodivergent. Breeding's empowering narrative inspires readers to challenge preconceived notions, foster empathy, and champion diversity in all its forms.

Whether you're a neurodivergent individual, a caregiver, or simply curious about the intricacies of the human mind, "Celebrating Neurodiversity" is a must-read that will leave a lasting impact. Join Travis Breeding on a journey of self-discovery, acceptance, and celebration as we embrace the kaleidoscope of neurodiversity and revel in the beauty of our differences.

Read more at breedingautismconsulting.com.

Also by Travis Breeding

Harmony in Flux: Navigating Bi-Polar Brilliance
The Friendship Rainbow
The Great Kindergarten Adventure: A Story about Going to School
with Autism
The Magic Forest Adventure
Unlocking Brilliance: Navigating Autism and Applied Behavior
Analysis Towards a Radiant Future
Decoding Love: Navigating Dating and Relationships on the Autism
Spectrum
Echoes of a Late Diagnosis: Unveiling the Spectrum Within
From Theory to Practice: Implementing Effective Autism Interventions
St
The Amazing Adventures of Aiden and His Asperger's Superpowers
The Magical Adventures of Lily and the Enchanted Forest
Unlocking Potential: A Journey Of Discovery Through ABA Therapy
Unlocking Potential: Navigating Employment for Neurodiverse Talent
Unlocking the Spectrum: A Journey through Applied Behavior Analysis
from an Autistic Perspective
Unlocking The Spectrum: Navigating The Complexity Of Autism With
Advanced Strategies And Insights
Beyond The Spectrum: Insights From Autistic Adults
Beyond The Stereotypes
Breaking Barriers: Navigating Autism With Therapeutic Insight
Celebrating Neurodiversity
Embracing Differences

About the Author

Travis is the author of over 50 books about autism spectrum disorder. He travelst he country sharing the mission of making the world a better place for autistic individuals. In his spare time Travis enjoys writing, walking, and watching sports.

Read more at breedingautismconsulting.com.